Implementing Training

The Competent Trainer's Toolkit Series
by David G. Reay

Implementing Training is the sixth 'tool' in the series. The first — *Understanding the Training Function* — stands outside the training cycle. The rest, including this book, deal with the cycle stage by stage, from planning your initial strategy right through to evaluating the contribution training makes to the prosperity of your organization.

All these books can be used on training courses or as aids to self-development.

Implementing Training

Training

DAVID G REAY

**Kogan Page Ltd, London
Nichols Publishing Company,
New Jersey**

Published in association with **OTSU** LIMITED

First published in 1994

Apart from any fair dealing for the purposes of research or private study, or criticism or review, as permitted under the Copyright, Designs and Patents Act, 1988, this publication may only be reproduced, stored or transmitted, in any form or by any means, with the prior permission in writing of the publishers, or in the case of reprographic reproduction in accordance with the terms of licences issued by the Copyright Licensing Agency. Enquiries concerning reproduction outside those terms should be sent to the publishers at the undermentioned address:

Kogan Page Limited
120 Pentonville Road
London N1 9JN

© OTSU Ltd 1994

Published in the United States of America by Nichols Publishing,
PO Box 6036, East Brunswick, New Jersey 08816

British Library Cataloguing in Publication Data

A CIP record of this book is available from the British Library.
ISBN: (UK) 0 7494 1287 9
ISBN: (US) 0-89397-428-5

Printed and bound in Great Britain by Biddles Ltd, Guildford and King's Lynn

Contents

Acknowledgements

This series is to a large extent based on OTSU's experiences during the past decade. Because of this, so many people have been involved in its formulation that it would be impossible to name them all. However, there are a number of people without whose help this series would not have seen the light of day.

I would like therefore to give my sincere thanks to Paul Leach for his constant support with writing, Adrian Spooner for his editing skill, Aidan Lynn for setting the series in motion, Jill Sharpe and Kathleen Gibson for design and desk-top publishing, Dorothy Reay and Amanda Froggatt for proof-reading and finally Dolores Black at Kogan Page who didn't mind flexible deadlines.

Introduction

Who this Book is For

As part of *The Competent Trainer's Toolkit Series*, this book is intended primarily for trainers and professionals involved in day-to-day training. If you are such a person I hope you will be able to identify with the scenes I portray and you are able to put into action some or all of the ideas I discuss.

However, I realize that the potential audience for this book is far wider than those people who would identify themselves immediately as training professionals. There are organizations where someone may need to arrange a course or a series of courses for their colleagues. Course organizers of such events could do worse than to dip into this book for ideas about what to do and what to avoid doing.

Also, anyone who needs to be sure they are getting the most out of the training method which they have selected should find this book to be of value. You may have decided for perfectly valid reasons that, say, computer-based training is the appropriate medium for you to work in. But that is not to say that you will necessarily use it to the best advantage.

The advantages to be gained from enhancing the performance of every area of your training are enormous. So trainers in organizations, large or small, who use a variety of training methods, will find this book particularly helpful.

This book is based on the experience of my colleagues and myself over the last ten years in Europe and America. In that time we have experienced training whose quality runs across the whole gamut from excellent to, well, let's be frank, abysmal. I'd like to think that this book will help your work move ever more firmly into the 'excellent' category.

So What is Implementing Training all About?

One point I make strongly throughout this series, but especially in Book 1, is that the existence of the training function is justified entirely by its contribution to the survival and prosperity of the organization. The most visible part of the training function's contribution is the way in which the training is implemented. And like most things in life the implementation can be done well or it can be done badly.

The advantages of high quality implementation are increased value for money for the organization and increased credibility and standing for yourself and the whole training function in the eyes of all your customers, be they board members, managers, staff or your own team. On the other hand the risks of doing it badly can be dire. Remember, the implementation of training is your most visible action. You can plan strategies, analyse needs, select methods and evaluate as successfully as you like; but if you fail to implement properly, everyone will notice and your standing will suffer. Conversely, of course, successful implementation can compensate to some degree for shortcomings in other areas.

A training needs analysis may reveal that your people need skills and attitude training in a certain area. The process of selecting training methods may reveal that certain methods are appropriate. But you also need to know what is involved in implementing the training so that you can decide whether it is appropriate to:

- proceed straight away with implementation — because you've got the skills and knowledge you need already available
- provide development for your trainers and then proceed to implement the training
- buy in training from providers who have the necessary skills.

Taken all in all, implementing training is not only a key element of your job it is the most visible part of it.

So getting it right is vital.

In our terms the way to get it right is to make sure you keep asking yourself — 'Will it help the learners to learn?'. As all learning takes place inside the heads of the learners the best you can hope to achieve is to provide the kinds of experiences which enable and encourage the learner to learn. And a large part of the experience is the way the training is implemented.

People learn best when they are active. That doesn't mean they have to be running or leaping around but they should be actively engaged in listening, questioning, analysing, synthesizing and making links between what they know, feel or do already and the state you are expecting them to reach.

You should consider all of these when you are deciding how to implement your training.

Objectives

By the time you have worked through this book, you will be able to:

- describe all you need to do when you choose and set up a location for group training

- apply the interpersonal and presentation skills you need when you are involved in group training

- set out the details of the preparation you need to make if side-by-side training is to be successful in your organization

- locate and select open learning materials

- decide when customized open learning materials are appropriate, and explain how to commission and develop them

- explain the support and evaluation structures required for successful open learning

- recognize the costs involved in computer-based training and interactive video

- describe the kinds of tasks and projects which form an effective basis for discovery learning

- create an organizational environment supportive of discovery learning.

Overview

To help you find your way round this book, there follows an overview of each chapter.

Chapter 1 — Group-based Training

This chapter begins with an analysis of the importance of accurate objective-setting in all group events and then moves on to deal with programme design, venue preparation and joining instructions. You will then proceed into the important areas of presentation skills and interpersonal skills. At the end of the chapter you'll explore the necessary steps to be taken after the training event is complete.

Chapter 2 — Side-by-side Training

This chapter deals first of all with the best ways of creating an environment where side-by-side training will flourish. Following this, you'll address ways of choosing people to be coaches and providing them with the development they need. After the next point, which is ways of developing training materials, you move into the areas of assessing and monitoring side-by-side training.

Chapter 3 — Text-based Open Learning

In this chapter you'll look at those factors which may make open learning suitable for your organization, where to find it, and how to make your own if there is none available off-the-shelf. You'll also look closely at the support which open learning needs to make it successful, and at the way you need to keep a check on individuals' progress.

Chapter 4 — Computer-based Training and Interactive Video

To get the best out of computer-based training and other highly sophisticated training delivery methods, you will need to work out the answers to various questions concerning, among other things, the delivery system and the nature of the support required. On a different track, but equally important, is the need to develop your training provision in this area. Both these topics are addressed in this chapter.

Chapter 5 — Discovery Learning

In this chapter you'll explore the practical actions you as a trainer will need to take if you are to enable learners to benefit from their discovery learning. Book 5 in this series, *Selecting Training Methods,* describes what discovery learning is — this chapter explains how you make each stage of the process work.

How to Use this Book

This is not a text which you will read once and then put away never to read again (I hope!). Its inclusion in the *Competent Trainer's Toolkit Series* indicates that it is designed for you to use in your work as a trainer.

How you work through the book is really up to you. You may, if you wish, work through the pages in order from front to back and cover the whole text in that way. The book is constructed logically so that you can work right through it. Alternatively you can dip into a chapter at a time, as and when you need to.

There is a range of activities and assignments for you to complete inside each chapter. Activities are distinguished by the fact that there is some feedback — not always in the form of right or wrong answers, because there are not always hard-and-fast right or wrong answers to be had. Assignments, on the other hand, are an opportunity for you to get out into your organization and ask some questions of yourself which will help you to see just how well you are implementing various training methods — and there are opportunities for you to spot ways of improving your performance.

As an additional benefit, by completing assignments you will be creating a body of evidence for your vocational qualification. You should keep this text and the outcomes of the activities and assignments as a record of your study.

Because the book calls on you to write your own thoughts and think about your own situation it will become your personal record and guide to the way you implement training.

You should feel free to write notes at any point in the margins or on the text. In fact, the more notes you write, the more useful this book will be to you in the long term.

Training and Development Lead Body Competences

Many trainers and training managers in the UK are actively seeking professional vocational qualifications, through the National Vocational Qualifications route. There are competences at level 3 and 4 of the NVQ in Training and Development for which you will be able to use this book as part of your portfolio of evidence.

I have prepared below, a matrix which matches a list of assignments in this book and the competences, published in autumn 1994, which appear in the scheme booklets provided by the awarding bodies. Simply tick off the numbered assignments as you do them. Then, when you've completed this book, you can include the book itself together with any supporting documents you may create as you work through it in your NVQ portfolio. This simple matching technique will allow your NVQ assessor easily to locate your evidence and match it against the relevant criteria. Each assignment goes towards meeting performance criteria outlined in the elements shown.

Assignment at end of Chapters	The Assignment Contains Evidence Towards these Elements								
1	B121	B122	B211	B212	B221	B222	B311	B312	B322	B331
	B332	C111	C232	C241	C261	C271	C272	E212	E221	E222
	E231	E232	E311							
2	B121	B122	B211	C111	C251	C252				
3	A212	A222	B212	B312	B322	B331	B332	C111	C212	C213
	C221	C222	C231	C252	C261	C262	C263	D111	D112	D113
	D311	D312	E211	E212	E213	E221	E222			
4	B112	B122	B321	B322	B323	B324				
5	B121	B122	B212	B222	B312	B331	B332	C111	C213	C232
	D111	E212	E221							

A212   Identify and agree individuals' learning requirements
A222   Identify learning needs with individuals
B112   Devise a strategy for training and development within an organization
B121   Select options for implementing training and development activities
B122   Develop a training and development implementation plan
B211   Select options for meeting learning requirements
B212   Design learning programmes for learners
B221   Identify options for meeting learning requirements
B222   Design training and development sessions for learners
B311   Agree requirements for training and development requirements
B312   Design training and development materials
B321   Agree requirements for information technology (IT) based training and development
materials with client
B322   Design information technology (IT) based training and development materials
B323   Test designs for information technology (IT) based training and development materials
B324   Modify designs for information technology (IT) based training and development materials
B331   Prepare materials and facilities to support learning
B332   Develop materials to support learning
C111   Agree roles and resources with contributors
C212   Support learners' needs
C213   Promote access to learning and achievement
C221   Negotiate learning programmes with learners
C222   Review learning programmes and agree modifications with learners
C231   Give presentations to groups
C232   Facilitate exercises and activities to promote learning in groups
C241   Demonstrate the skills and methods to learners
C251   Coach individual learners
C252   Assist individual learners to apply their learning
C261   Provide guidance to help individual learners plan their learning
C262   Agree the roles and resources required to support the achievement of individual learning
C263   Advise and support individual learners in managing their own learning
C271   Manage group dynamics
C272   Facilitate collaborative learning
D111   Collect information on learners' progress
D112   Conduct formative assessments with learners
D113   Review progress with learners
D311   Design instruments for the collection of performance evidence
D312   Design instruments for the collection of knowledge evidence
E211   Select methods for evaluating training and development programmes
E212   Collect information to evaluate training and development programmes
E213   Analyse information to improve training and development programmes
E221   Identify potential improvements to training and development programmes
E222   Plan the introduction of improvements to training and development programmes
E231   Collect and analyse information on training and development sessions
E232   Improve training and development sessions
E311   Evaluate own practice

Group-based Training

Given its popularity, not only in the UK but in the training scene worldwide, it's not surprising that we're presenting group-based training first. Training is group-based for many people, and, if it's selected as a method for the right reasons and implemented well, it can be enormously successful as a medium for facilitating learning.

By the time you have worked through this chapter, you will be able to:

- describe the stages which have to be gone through before a training event takes place:
  — objectives setting
  — programme design
- explain the criteria to be observed when you sort out your location, the venue and the equipment you need
- prepare appropriate joining instructions
- analyse and improve your presentation skills
- analyse and improve your interpersonal skills
- arrange appropriate follow-up to a group-based training course.

Group-based training covers all training where two or more people are learning together — so there is a lot of ground to cover. We'll make a start.

Setting Objectives

The best trainers never forget the need to make training **relevant** — to the organization, to the learner and to the job.

Ensuring relevance starts early on in the training cycle: **everything** the training function does must be relevant to the organization's needs; the training strategy should match organizational and individual objectives; the training provision must match learning styles.

By this stage, you may be wondering what more you can do to make training relevant when it comes to the detail of planning a training event. The answer lies in knowing that the training you provide is based on **objectives which accurately reflect the needs you've identified**. That may sound obvious, but it's all too easy to get it wrong by using convenient shorthand when you design your training. Let's take an example.

Imagine for a moment that your organization has recognized that first-line supervisors are not controlling staff overtime properly. Some more research shows that this is because they don't understand the monthly financial statements they receive. You are asked to include this in the introductory courses you run for newly-appointed supervisors. For convenience, you include this under the heading 'Monthly Financial Statements'.

Why is this session on 'Monthly Financial Statements' in danger of not meeting the real training need? Write your answers in here.

We thought of three reasons. **First**, the inclusion of this session in training for newly-appointed supervisors will not meet the need for supervisors already in the post.

Second, the terse heading 'Monthly Financial Statements' is not specific enough about the **level** of training. Does it mean:

- a superficial understanding of where they come from and how they are produced?
- an appreciation of how the organization controls its finances?
- a practical grasp of the information included in the statements and how it can be applied?
- a combination of these, or something different again?

All of which brings us on to our third concern. To be effective, training must be based on a clear statement of:

- precisely what the trainee should be able to do following the training
- under what conditions

  and
- to what standard.

In training terms that's what objectives mean. Look at each of these points in turn.

What Should People be able to do Following the Training?

All we've been saying so far about making training relevant should make it obvious that the answer to this question has to be 'perform their jobs better'. The trouble is that training alone can't achieve that. Training furnishes learners with the opportunity to acquire knowledge, skills and attitudes which in turn give them the **potential** to perform better. Whether they actually perform better depends on the resources, support and conditions in the workplace.

Therefore training objectives — while they must be about learners doing things — must be restricted so that when you measure whether they've been achieved or not, you get accurate results, not corrupted by workplace factors.

Taking the supervisors you read about on page 16 for an example, what sort of objectives could you construct which would involve learner activity, but not involve workplace factors? Write two or three in here.

There are a number of possible angles to this one. Here are a few of the possibilities we thought of.

At the end of their training, supervisors will be able to:

- calculate variance to budget from the 'Monthly Financial Statement'
- recognize where overtime payments have exceeded the budget provision
- project likely overspends from expenditure trends to date
- suggest ways of controlling overtime payments so that expenditure does not exceed budget.

It's important to recognize that all of these possible objectives start with **doing** verbs. The technical term for this is 'observable behaviours'. In other words, once the training has been completed, the trainer will be able to see if it has been successful. Can people now do what the training set out to achieve? Evaluation of training is an important topic in it's own right and is dealt with in *Evaluating Training*, book 7 in this series.

Under What Conditions

It wouldn't be enough to ask someone 'Can I get from here to the next town in an hour?'. You'd have to be specific and say whether you meant by car, bus, bike or on foot. In the same way, training objectives need to take account of and state clearly the resources the learner will need to complete the task and the environment in which they will operate. So, for example, we'd have to decide whether our supervisors will have access to a calculator or to pencil and paper when calculating variances to budget. If we're setting a performance standard for typists, we'd have to specify whether they'd be using manual or electronic typewriters or word-processors. Performance standards for tyre-fitters will vary according to whether they're working in a fitting-bay, or at the side of the road, with the wheel on or off the car. In each case, the level of difficulty and perhaps even the knowledge and skill required, will vary.

To What Standard?

So far, we've defined training objectives in terms of **what** is to be done. We haven't said anything about **how well,** though. This is easier for some jobs than for others. We can qualify shorthand or typing speeds by reference to words per minute and percentage errors. A description of a manual task must include a reference to how long the task should take and a clear statement of the accepted levels of tolerance. Interpersonal skills like personal selling or interviewing are more difficult, but even in these cases a measurable standard can be defined by breaking-down a complex skill into simpler elements and monitoring how many elements are achieved. For example, the standard of salesmanship can be measured by observing whether the salesman:

- asks qualifying questions
- identifies a suitable product
- sells the benefits
- closes the sale.

The more detailed your breakdown of the skill into elements, the easier it is to recognize whether each element has been performed.

What this means for you

Objectives need to specify:

- observable behaviours
- the conditions under which they are to be achieved

  and
- the standard to be reached.

From this it is clear that it takes a lot of time and trouble to get objectives right. Have a go yourself, now.

Think of two tasks with which you are familiar in your organization. Now write down a training objective related to each one. Make sure you include behaviour, conditions and standard for each. Write your answer in this grid.

Task being trained for	Behaviour	Conditions	Standard
1.			
2.			

Here are a few examples from our experience:

Task being trained for	Behaviour	Conditions	Standard
Servo overhaul	Strip down a vacuum servo, replace seals and assemble	At workbench with necessary tools within 35 minutes	The overhauled servo works correctly
Accident awareness	Write down the ten most frequent accidents in our organization	In 20 minutes	To 90% accuracy
Fire alarm procedure	Describe the six actions to take in case of fire alarm	To the trainer's satisfaction under training conditions	To 100% accuracy
Piston wear assessment	Measure the wear on a piston	Using piston and still rule	To a tolerance of 3%

Writing objectives for every element of training is a potentially time-consuming job. But remember that carefully constructed objectives are the only way to ensure that the training is a good match with identified needs. Without them, too, you have no way of measuring whether the training has been effective. They also provide an essential framework for making sure a training programme covers everything it ought to cover. That's the area we'll look at next.

Designing the Programme

Learning objectives are an essential startpoint for any kind of training, be it group-based, side-by-side, open learning, computer-based training, interactive video, or discovery learning. We'll be referring back to them at several points in this book. In this section of this chapter, we'll be concentrating on programme design as it relates specifically to group training. Other forms of training need slightly different approaches, as you'll see later.

Group training may last for hours, days or weeks. Whichever is the case, you'll probably be faced with the same kind of panic as you sit down with a set of learning objectives and a blank sheet of paper.

We'd encourage you to start by thinking about your learners. Only if you put yourself in the position of your learners and identify with them will you be able to design a programme from which your people will derive maximum benefit. A good way of focusing your mind is to concentrate on the hopes, fears and expectations you think your learners are likely to have for the course.

What might be the hopes, fears and expectations of a group of learners before attempting a training course? Write your answer in this box please.

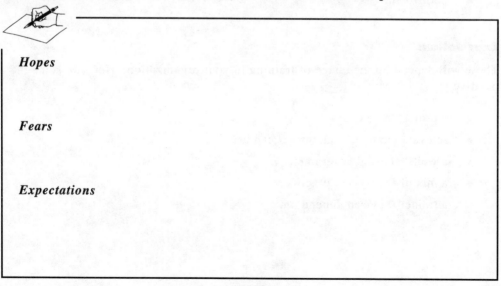

Hopes

Fears

Expectations

Here are some of the main things course members have said to us most frequently about a wide range of courses:

Hopes

- to have a good time
- to meet friends and colleagues
- to be stimulated
- to learn something new and useful.

Fears

- being made to look foolish
- not understanding
- failing
- not keeping up with the others
- being bored
- uncomfortable seats
- poor food.

Expectations

These will depend on the image of training in your organization. Here are some positive possibilities:

- a professional course
- relevant content, something I can use
- a well-balanced programme
- a mix of theory and practice
- a trainer they can depend on.

Of course, in an organization where a poor image of training exists, trainees' expectations would almost certainly throw up the exact opposites of these.

So how can we use these hopes, fears and expectations as a basis for programme design? It will help you to think of your training as a product. If your learners are to 'buy into' your product, it will have to:

- fulfil their hopes
- live up to their positive expectations
- banish their fears
- disprove their negative expectations.

In other words, your training will have to meet your consumers' **needs**. There are, in the training environment, two kinds of needs.

What must a training programme include to meet the training needs and customer needs of your course members? Write a list here. Just use headings for now, we'll provide the details over the next few pages.

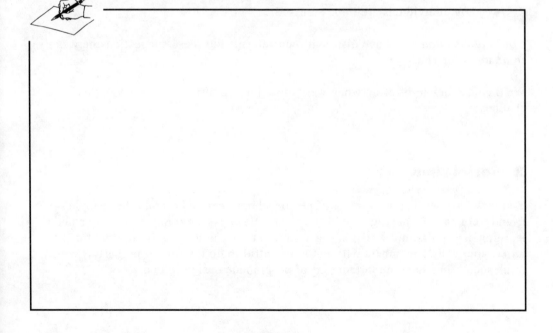

We found that there was a measure of overlap between a lot of the things we wanted to include. So we've just listed them here, in no particular order.

1   Clear Briefing and Introductions

Do you remember people's fears of not understanding or of looking foolish? And their hopes and expectations of something useful and relevant from a trainer they can depend on? A lot of these factors can be tackled right at the start of a course by including a clear briefing and introduction. We always include these pieces of information on our courses:

- the objectives of the programme
- the timetable
- practical details: toilets, meal arrangements, coffee breaks
- in case of difficulty: who to contact, what to do
- the style of the course: flexible, participative, activity-based
- how individuals are to be assessed.

Your organization may have different requirements but these suggestions may spark some ideas for you.

We'll come back to briefing when we look at joining instructions later in this chapter.

2   Social Time

You may have noticed how many of people's hopes centred round other people — friends, colleagues, having a good time. Strictly speaking training should be about learning new skills, not gossiping in the bar, but if you don't build in time for the latter, your course members will be too resentful to do the former properly. We think social time is an important part of programme design in two ways:

a   Getting to know people

If you're going to spend time — anything from a few hours to several weeks — with a group of people, you want to know about them; for example, their experience, strengths and weaknesses, hobbies and interests. Curiosity is a natural human emotion, so the sooner you can get this kind of information out on the table, the sooner people will turn to your agenda. The important thing to remember, though, is to be realistic about the time it takes and to allow that time. You should encourage people to open up about themselves, but be careful not to pry into private areas.

b   Training as real life

As trainers, you could sometimes get so single-minded that you would resent anything that detracted from your training priority. So you would disapprove of any conversation that wasn't directly relevant to the last session and 'talk shop' yourself to the exclusion of everything else.

The reality is very different. If your training is relevant and stimulating, course members will automatically talk about how they can apply it to their own jobs. You can't force that kind of conversation, but you need to include social time during which it can happen.

You also want your course members to see training as a natural part of their lives. So, at coffee and over lunch, it fits comfortably alongside discussion of who got the latest promotion and the next social club outing. Social time lets the real world of work into the training programme. Both should benefit as a result.

3   Review and Consolidation

There is such a thing as a single-minded trainer, who wants to cram as much training into a course as he or she possible can. A further risk they run is that their course members never have time to step back mentally and think about what they're doing. An effective training programme needs to include space and time for regular reviews of learning. Course members should be encouraged to think through questions like:

- What have I just learned?

- What will I do differently as a result?

- What implications does it have for other parts of my job?

- What are the benefits?

You'll be able to add more questions of your own. This process needs to be handled sensitively. Set time aside for it, but be ready to introduce it as a different item, if you sense the need. And — **don't use a checklist!** Reviews should challenge course members to think about their learning. You will challenge each new group with a different set of questions each time. Careful tailoring of reviews is a crucial part of making training relevant. But there are also implications for you as trainers. Put simply, you have to **listen** to what people say and **remember** it. Although it's put simply, it's difficult to do in the heat of a group event. So you might decide to have two presenters each of whom takes on a different role, one facilitating and one making notes or comments, watching expressions and so on.

4 Variety

The typical attention span of a typical course member is just 20 minutes! That makes it vital to build change and variety into a programme. From your own knowledge of your target group and of the training objectives, you can decide how long they need on one subject. Let's say you decide to include a two-hour session on health and safety.

Now think of all the different ways you could use that time. Write your ideas here:

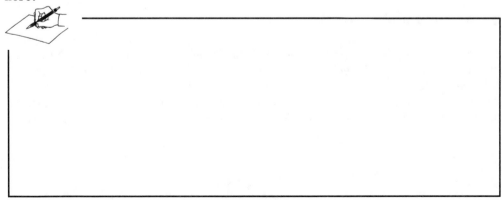

These are some we thought of:

- lecture
- discussion
- film
- slides
- individual assessment

- team quiz
- group exercise
- game
- simulation
- role play.

Of course, you can't include them all. People need time to alter pace and activity. But we'd definitely encourage you to ring the changes as much as you practically can. That will help meet course members' needs for interest and stimulation. It'll also help meet the training objectives. Variety helps people's learning by constantly keeping them alert and thus extending their concentration span. In the literature you'll see this referred to as the Hawthorne Effect. I've even heard trainers dismissing others' successes as only working because of the Hawthorne Effect. My response, is 'So what?'. If you can encourage people to learn by being different then do it. Using the Hawthorne Effect well is called 'avoiding being boring'. It's certainly not cheating.

A final benefit — you can use different activities to get people up, moving, off their chairs! Sitting down for a day is foreign to many course members. The more active their normal jobs, the more difficult they will find it to sit still and learn.

5 Flexibility

We said earlier that you ought to explain the timetable as part of your course introduction. Now we're saying the course programme should be flexible. But the contradiction is only superficial. Our suggestion here is that you should design your programme in blocks of time big enough for you to move things around inside them. For instance a typical training day will give four time blocks of one-and-a-half hours: start-time till coffee, coffee till lunch, lunch till tea, tea till close. Of course, you need objectives and an outline for each of those blocks. But your learners will respond and learn much better if you let them take the session where they want it to go. An example may help.

Case Study

> On a recent group team-building event, I prepared a detailed scenario in which the team members were to get involved. I put the group under a good deal of time pressure to reach a decision regarding choices of who was to live and die in a fictitious situation.
>
> Two minutes into the activity, one person noted that the activity resembled very much a situation the team had encounted the previous week concerning staff lay-offs. During the ensuing (unplanned) discussion, the team talked about how each member had performed in the recent crisis, and spent the next hour coming to an awareness of the importance of different roles in the team — which, coincidentally, had been the objective of my fictitious scenario. They reached the original objective but by a route I could not have predicted in advance.

This shows the session achieving its objective, but taking in a few other directly relevant topics on the way, because that's what the course members wanted to talk about. We're back to our theme of relevance and usefulness again!

If you're new to training, the idea of not being in total control of a group session may fill you with horror. If you feel more relaxed and confident with a tightly-structured programme, you'll be a better trainer if you have one. But you will find it helps to develop the ability to handle some flexibility. Try following a group comment which extends part of an objective and see what ensues. Over time, your confidence in following comments from the group will grow, along with your store of visuals, exercises and anecdotes to support flexibility. Eventually you'll reach the point where you can provide exactly what's relevant to the group and leave 90 per cent of your notes and source materials behind. That's when you can feel really in control.

6 Time to Absorb

We remember attending a course which was led by one of the most knowledgeable, experienced, dynamic and resourceful trainers we've ever met. From 8 o'clock in the morning till the bar closed at night, we discussed training management, for a whole week. Unfortunately, it was just too much. By Wednesday, our collective brains were full to bursting. We'd reached the point of information overload: we couldn't absorb any more.

So part of programme design is recognizing when people need private time to consider what they've been learning. That may mean finishing a session at 12.30 instead of 1.00. Or telling the group to go for a walk for 10 minutes. Or building-in a longer coffee-break. Or even giving the course a free evening. Course members need time and space to ponder the training. Time set aside deliberately for that purpose will mean they're willing and able to concentrate on what comes afterwards. Without it they won't be. What you're doing is allowing people time to consolidate and restructure for themselves the experiences they've been having.

Conclusion

There's no such thing as an ideal programme structure. Only you can say in detail what will suit your groups, your objectives and your organization. But we believe that your programmes will be much better at meeting both the training and the customer needs of your course members if you build in briefing, social time, reviews, variety, flexibility and time to absorb in the ways we've been describing.

Considering the Venue

You may have no choice as to where you run your training sessions. If the organization has a training centre, or a training room, which you are expected to use, you may have to apply some of this book backwards. In other words, if the book says you need a resource you haven't got for a particular training method, you'll have to find an alternative approach for which the resources are available. If, on the other hand, you are responsible for finding a training venue, a lot of choices come along with this freedom.

What factors would you consider when deciding on a training venue? Think about the needs of the training itself, the course members and your organization.

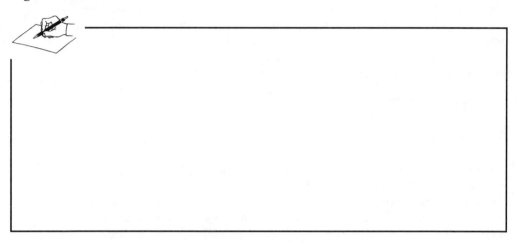

Here is our own list of factors:

- availability and size of rooms
- transport arrangements
- availability of equipment
- room layout
- meals and speed of service
- noise levels
- experience and expertise

You should look at each factor now in greater detail.

Availability and Size of Rooms

If the session you're planning is a short briefing, you'll probably only need one room. In that case, your concerns will be limited to making sure it's big enough (beware! Some hotels are optimistic to say the least about the number of people who can be seated in their conference rooms) and that entrances and exits are convenient and clearly signposted.

If, on the other hand, you're planning a longer, more varied course, you'll probably want to include some syndicate activity, discussions, case-study work and so on. That means a main room and a number of syndicate rooms. Remember that it helps to have syndicate rooms close to the main room, particularly if your course is going to break frequently for short activities. If syndicate work will be lengthy, the location of the rooms is less important, but the size is crucial. Expecting six people to work for several days in a room which is normally a single bedroom is asking for trouble!

Transport Arrangements

One fundamental question that's easy to overlook is, 'Where are my course members coming from and how will they get to the course?'. If everyone will come by car, is the car park big enough? Can you reserve spaces? How close is the railway station? Is there a good-sized taxi rank? How frequent are the buses? This is just another aspect of considering your training from the customer's viewpoint. And do remember, if your course members haven't been to this location before, they'll need a map that's accurate and easy to read.

Availability of Equipment

Your organization may provide you with mobile equipment, OHPs, film projectors and so on to take with you when you run courses away from base. This means you can be sure it's available, but do check it over when you arrive to make sure it hasn't been damaged on the way.

Alternatively, you may expect the venue to provide it for you. Most places say they can provide the normal range of equipment, but do check:

- that they've got enough for all the conferences running that day
- that it's of a type and standard you're comfortable with
- that you can afford the hire charges.

Room — Layout and Fixed Points

Different styles and methods of training work best with different room layouts. For example, discussions tend to work best with chairs in a circle and no desks. If you want people to make notes they'll need at least a writing-tray and for lengthy written exercises they will need desks. If you think about the most effective layout for the methods you want to use, you'll be able to check possible rooms against these criteria.

Flexibility of layout will often depend on the position of fixed points in the room. By this we mean things like power points, light switches, the fixed screen and even the windows. This diagram illustrates an extreme case:

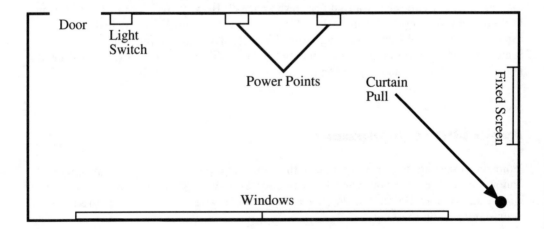

It is ideally equipped for a training event using tables laid out in a U-shape with the open end towards the screen. All those seated would get a good view. An OHP could also be used easily in this arrangement. If the trainer wants to use a film projector, though, the cable will have to run across the middle of the room because the screen is fixed. If the trainer sets up the projector at power points, he or she can't get to the curtain pull and even the light switch is difficult. We could go on, but you'll have begun to see how some rooms will suit the sort of training you want to do, while others will not.

Meal-times and Speed of Service

We think it's important that meal, coffee and tea breaks should fit in with the training, not the other way round. So our ideal is a situation where the course can break at any stage between two predetermined times and people can eat or drink then. It's equally important to be able to restart when you want to, not when the restaurant staff have finished serving. We've come across places where you had to allow two hours for lunch because that's how long it took to serve three courses and coffee!

So it helps, when you're considering a possible venue, to find out if coffee and tea can be served in a separate area, to be taken when you're ready for it. Does the venue have a self-service arrangement for lunches? If not, how quickly do the restaurant staff serve? Remember, too, that heavy lunches tend to send people to sleep! Would a light soup-or-salad meal help concentration in the afternoon? If so, is one available?

Noise-levels

There can be a whole host of sources of noise which are easy to overlook, but which can destroy a training session. Here are a number of check questions to think about, some obvious, some less so:

- Are the training rooms on a busy corridor?
- When do the cleaning staff use the vacuum-cleaners?

- How near the bar are you?

- Are you close to a fire-door or external door which bangs or squeaks?

- How close are the rooms to a main road?

- Do you overlook a lawn? If so, how noisy is the lawn mower?

- If you checked the room in winter, how noisy will it be in summer with the windows open?

- What is scheduled to happen in the room next to yours? (Dance? Film show? Talent contest? Public Speaking Course? Brainstorming session?)

Experience and Expertise

There is an unalterable law which states that if anything can go wrong, it will. In training that may mean a bulb blowing, running out of paper, an unexpected need for extra photocopies or a session that overruns wildly. A venue that's used to training should be able to take all of this — and worse — in its stride. It will have the facilities and resources you need to hand because it will have had experience of training and will understand what's needed. The best way to check the level of experience and expertise which your venue organizers possess is to raise some 'What if . . .?' questions. Ask your contact to explain what happens if . . .

- you need a coffee half-an-hour early?
- the OHP packs up?
- one of your course members goes sick?
- you need an exercise typed and copied?
- you run out of flipchart paper?

The answers should convey the feeling that all these events are routine and expected, not the cause of a sudden panic.

Cost

We've left this consideration deliberately till last because we believe that, while it's important, several of the things we've already mentioned are more so. Nevertheless you should give costs some careful thought — and not just the obvious ones. Make sure you know what's included in the room hire and what isn't. Are syndicate rooms extra or included? Does coffee come with biscuits or without? Think about your course members, too. What are bar prices like? Does the room rate cover morning tea and a newspaper? But don't forget: a cheap second-rate venue will earn you a much worse press than a dearer, quality one.

Joining Instructions

Throughout this series, we've stressed the need for training to be a joint undertaking between line management and the training function. Giving people advance details of the course they're about to attend is a prime example of this cooperation. Use the next activity to think about what both line managers and course members need to know in advance.

What does a course member need from joining instructions? What does the line manager need from joining instructions? Answer both those questions in this box.

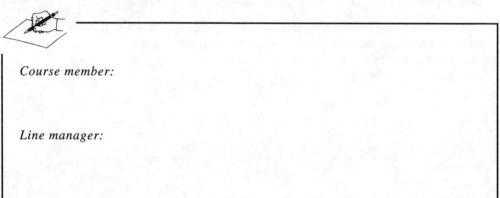

Course member:

Line manager:

The Course Member

We thought the course member needed to know:

- the learning objectives and outline programme
- the starting date and training times
- the venue address along with the travel details we've already talked about
- any details of things each person should bring
- when there will be free time, and what leisure and sport facilities there might be.

You should always remember that some course members will have special needs. Access to the training facility may be difficult for some, and others may need a speical diet. You must give course members an opportunity to register special requests before the course begins.

The Line Manager

Naturally, the line manager needs to know what the course member has been told about the course they're going to. After all, if you want the line manager committed to the training process, it's a good idea not to bypass them when you send out course information!

In addition, we thought the line manager might appreciate some help with briefing. After all, passing on all the information about a course is a skilled activity and needs accurate and accessible materials to work from.

Case Study

Jeff Mandell ran the administration team at Gracefield Hospital. He used to resent junior administrators going on courses for four reasons:

- no one ever told him any details
- the trainees went on the course not knowing what to expect
- they came back to work thoroughly informed about minor issues and ignorant of major ones
- they gave him the impression that what they had learnt was more important than what they actually did in the course of their job.

When the new training manager issued joining instruction to trainees and copied them to him, he immediately felt involved. When the trainer sent guidelines suggesting ways in which Jeff could prepare trainees for the course — discussing with them which learning points were crucial in terms of each trainee's personal objectives — Jeff became a committed supporter of training initiatives.

All you need to do to help a line manager with briefing his or her team is to point out some general aspects of the course which should be brought to the attention of trainees. You should also remind line managers of the need to agree personal objectives with each of their staff members.

Timing for Joining Instructions

Within reason, we reckon the sooner you can send out joining instructions, the better. If managers and course members are to prepare together for the course, they will need time.

You'll probably need some information back from the manager and course member: confirmation of briefing, details of travel arrangements, possibly a statement from each trainee about their individual learning priorities for the course.

Add to all this a possible need for people to do some pre-course preparation — reading a case-study, perhaps, or completing a questionnaire — and you'll understand why we believe that joining instructions should go out anything between one and two months in advance of a course.

Equipment and Materials

Most trainers have some training aids they particularly like and others they prefer to avoid. The chances are that you're no different — so what do you do about it, given that an all-round competent trainer is more use than one with narrower competences who is on the verge of becoming a specialist?

Well, first — here's what you never do. You never restrict the training objectives you are supposed to meet just because you personally are uncomfortable with the materials and equipment you need to use. For example, you can't say:

- 'I'm not training people in 'face-the-media' techniques because I don't like handling video cameras'.

So — going back to first principles — what do you do to ensure your use of equipment and materials meets trainees' needs? Write a four-stage procedure here.

You should:

- draw up a list of the range of equipment and materials available
- draw up a list of the objectives of a specific course
- match the objective to the most appropriate equipment and materials you have at your disposal
- practise using those materials.

If the final step is impossible given the time-scales you've set yourself, then the straight fact is that your time-scales are too short. All is not lost, however; as a temporary measure you can get a colleague or a consultant to deliver the course for you using the necessary equipment.

Remember to leave time, too, for the preparation of materials. Handouts, acetates, exercise briefs can all be quickly prepared if you're happy with a series of words on paper. But if you want to entertain, inspire and involve your course members, materials design and preparation will take a lot longer.

Interim Review

There are so many things to consider when arranging a group training event that we should take this opportunity to review all you've looked at so far.

The preparation for a successful group training event involves:

- setting relevant objectives
- designing a programme which will meet those objectives effectively
- issuing appropriate joining instructions to course members — and sending copies to line managers, with hints about briefing
- arranging a suitable venue
- arranging suitable materials and equipment, and preparing yourself to use them.

So, the preparations are complete. But remember, however carefully you plan and prepare, you'll still need to be flexible.

The most important thing during the event is the relationship between the trainer and the group. The relationship depends on two sets of skills: the skill of presentation and interpersonal skills. We discuss these next.

Presentation Skills

Group presentation is a very practical skill. So the only way you can really improve it is by trying it, getting it wrong then learning from your mistakes. An open learning package like this one can do no more than provide some hints as to best practice — we must leave it to you to have a go for yourself! But here are the techniques that we've found useful.

Remember Course Members are Individuals

When we first stand up in front of a group of learners, we're sometimes petrified by that sea of anonymous faces. You'd be happy talking to any of them as individuals, so don't be frightened of an early silence. Instead, use that time to look briefly at each one of your course members — try to see a face, a personality, someone who's on your side, if only because they know how they'd feel if they were standing where you are!

Remember, too, that each member of your group is expecting to benefit personally from the course. So paying attention to them as individuals as the course progresses helps them think that you're working to help them alone. And of course, they're all different. You'll need to be aware of one person who's being left behind, or getting bored, or disagreeing silently, then you'll need to slow things down, start a discussion or issue a challenge to involve that individual.

Communicate with Care

We've said that a trainer's task is to get people to change the way they do things. To achieve that, the trainer needs to communicate effectively.

What should a trainer do to make communication effective? Write down three major features here.

-

-

-

We thought of four main ideas. See how yours compare to ours, remembering that you're unlikely to have used exactly our form of words.

Gain Feedback

Communication is only effective when you know how people have heard, understood and agreed with you. Feedback is the way you find out these things. It can come in several different ways:

- you ask questions, people respond
- people nod as you talk
- people show interest, or boredom, by how they sit or look
- you can set exercises and check the answers.

Remember Non-verbal Communication

We've already touched on this one, but do remember that you send messages to people, not just through the words you use, but also:

- by your tone of voice
- the way you put emphasis on particular phrases
  and
- through your body language.

You may **say** that something is very exciting, but if your voice sounds bored and you stare out of the window, no one will believe you. So watch for body language in others and make sure you give the same message with your body as you do with your voice.

Be Sensitive to the Mood of the Course

This is part of gaining feedback, but such an important part we thought it worth setting out on its own.

You can expect your course members to be a reasonably polite bunch — if your joining instructions have done their job and if they've been briefed properly, they'll have a good idea of what to expect from the course and they'll be ready to demonstrate commitment and keenness to learn. Besides this, you'll be a bit of an authority figure, anyway.

All this conspires to create a situation where they may not **tell** you when they're too tired to go on, or feeling uncomfortable, or have hit one of those 'lows' which can happen at any time, for all sorts of reasons. That's why it's important for you to be sensitive to the way people are feeling — and to be flexible enough to respond positively when things aren't going right. That means doing things like finishing early for lunch or coffee, changing the pace or the activity or even asking the group to explain how they're feeling and why. An informal review like this will give you powerful feedback on your style, or the relevance of the subject, or perhaps on the programme design. Whatever the outcome, you should be able to make productive use of it.

Use the Tools of the Trade

As a trainer, you have two main tools — your voice and your body. But they are both capable of an immense range of activities and the secret of effective group training is, we believe, to recognize the variety that you have available and make good use of it.

Let's think about your voice, first of all. Most of us are lazy about speaking. Our voices are often monotonous, with no variation of pitch or pace. And yet we can, if we practise, use our voices to attract and retain attention, to create interest and suspense, to emphasize points and ensure they're remembered. Here are a few techniques to practise:

- If people aren't paying attention, speak softly. They'll notice and strain to listen

- Pause for effect before main points
- Vary the pace and pitch of your voice to add interest
- Slow down and lower the tone of your voice for emphasis.

If you think these sound like an actor's techniques you'd be right. We don't think a trainer should try to be somebody different in front of a group, but we do believe he or she should be just a bit larger-than-life. After all, talking to a roomful of people isn't a natural activity. To be effective at it you need to be a bit unnatural as well.

The same applies to the ways we use our bodies. People learn much better when they hear and see things together. So you can use gestures and body movements to reinforce what you say. As with your voice, you need to think about the gestures you make and exaggerate slightly for effect. Whether you're pointing to a visual or counting on your fingers, your gestures need to be on a grand scale and slowed down a bit, so that everyone can see and take in the point you're making.

We'd call our final technique 'the lighthouse'. We said earlier it was important to treat course members as individuals — and to be seen to do so. One way of doing this is to train yourself to sweep your eyes and your head regularly from one side of the group to the other stopping briefly to make eye contact with each member on the way. Doing that means you can see whether individuals are interested, attentive, bored or asleep. And they see you taking a personal interest in each of them!

Interpersonal Skills

We've already looked at effective communication as one of the key presentation skills. But a trainer needs a much wider range of people skills than just this one and, for the purpose of this chapter, we'll classify all the other skills broadly as interpersonal skills.

What interpersonal skills do you feel are essential for an effective group trainer? List three here.

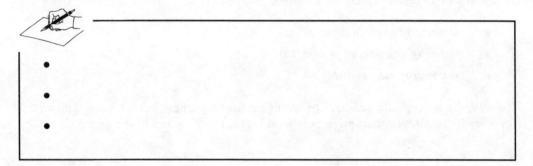

-
-
-

We latched onto these key skills.

Selecting a Style

Your 'style' covers not only the things you say and the way you say them, but also the clothes you wear and the way you wear them. We can't make recommendations which will suit everyone, but we can advise you to bear in mind the age and experience of your audience and the culture of your organization.

Assertiveness

You need to be in control of your group, but not to dominate it altogether. The key to success is leaving your emotions out of it. If you like what the group is doing and it's heading towards achieving the objectives, then fine. Take a back seat for a while. If you don't like it, because it's wrong and going off course:

- tell the group you disagree
- tell them exactly why you disagree.

If you don't like a group member's attitude and behaviour:

- ask them to explain themselves
- state why you accept or reject it
- take appropriate action.

Usually, the appropriate action is to arrange a friendly truce, but it's not unknown for a leader to ask one disruptive person to leave, for the good of the group.

Maintaining a Rapport

A successful training rapport is always based on mutual respect. **Your** end of the bargain is always to:

- seek
- respect
- respond to

others' contributions to the training session. Even if people are misguided and wrong in what they say, there are none the less ways of responding respectfully:

- 'I see what makes you feel like that . . . '
- 'A number of people think like that . . . '.

Of course, you add the 'but'; the key thing is you haven't been dismissive and rude, and you have affirmed the person's right to have opinions and to express them.

Interim Review

In the early part of this chapter you saw how to prepare for group-based training.

Over the last few pages you've looked at the skills you need when you are implementing a group training event — we broke them down into presentation skills and interpersonal skills.

Now it is time move on to the next stage — the things you need to do **after** the event.

After the Event

If your job involves running group training courses, your responsibility doesn't finish as the last course member walks out of the door. We believe that the things that happen **after** the course are closely linked to what happens **before** and **during** it.

All training should start with a set of training needs — things people need to be able to do but can't. Needs lead directly to the behavioural objectives which are designed into a training programme, after which people go back to work. Expressed like that, we hope you'll see how important it is for action to be taken:

- to see if course members can do the job you've trained them to do
- to help them apply the lessons of training to the real work.

We look in detail at the validation and evaluation of training in *Evaluating Training*, book 7 in this series. For the moment, we'll concentrate on helping course members make the transfer back to their normal work. Here are a few suggestions.

Personal Action Plans

These involve course members deciding, at the end of the course, those aspects which have been most relevant to them and the actions they will take as a result. Formal action plans should include a measure of achievement and a time-scale. These allow a trainer or line manager to review them with the course member.

Supervision

Increasingly, people are coming to expect feedback on how well they are performing. That means course members will welcome a regular opportunity to review performance with a senior colleague or supervisor. Of course, this needs to be someone who is well-known to the course member and trusted by them. It could be that the trainee's line manager will fit the bill, but remember this: always check with line managers when a trainee returns to work so that:

- the line managers allow time for one-to-one contact with the trainees
- they are not going to 'undo' any of your training by suggesting 'alternative' working methods.

Summary

In the course of Chapter 1 you've had a chance to examine a lot of the practicalities you need to consider when you're implementing group-based training.

First came the need for clear objectives, which have to be drawn up at the outset — other training methods rely just as heavily on good objectives, as you'll see in the rest of this book.

Second came the important matter of programme design. Good programme design accommodates the needs of the learners both as customers of your training function and as trainees. You saw that common elements included:

- clear briefings and introductions
- effective use of social time
- reviews and opportunities for consolidation
- variety
- flexibility
- time and opportunity to absorb information.

Third came matters of location and venue. Under this heading we looked at:

- rooms
- transport
- equipment
- meals
- noise levels
- availability of support.

Fourth came the significant detail of joining instructions, and the effect that these can have on trainees and line managers.

Fifth you looked at the range of equipment you may choose to use during your group training sessions.

The sixth point related to the presentation skills you will need, and there were lots of practical hints as to ways you can improve your performance in this area.

Seventh came interpersonal skills. Examining your training course from the trainees' perspective gave you an opportunity to focus on exactly what you were going to have to do to get the best out of them and enable them to achieve the most for themselves.

Last but not least was the series of steps you need to take to follow-up a group training course.

Assignment:

Use the headings and sub-headings you've seen in this chapter to make a checklist. For your next group-based training course, write down against each item on the checklist:

● *what you do.*

Leave some space after each item so that you can write down during and after the event:

● *how that particular aspect of your course and its preparations went*
● *what (if anything) you would do differently next time.*

You will notice that this assignment eventually builds into an action plan for you to follow throughout your preparation for all future group-based training exercises.

Side-by-side Training

Side-by-side training is a method of individual training in which the trainer encourages the learner to acquire new skills and habits in a practical way by practising them under the trainer's guidance and supervision.

When you design your side-by-side training, you will, of course, have to go through the familiar, formal steps of analysing tasks, setting objectives, deciding on instructional design and setting up evaluation systems. And when all that is done, you can start thinking about implementation.

By the time you have completed this chapter, you will be able to:

- describe an ideal environment for side-by-side training
- show how you would go about choosing and developing coaches
- explain how you would develop training materials
- apply the principles of assessment and monitoring.

One of the key points in this chapter is that side-by-side training doesn't just happen. Look at your office or workshop and you'll see people learning from each other all the time, picking up good and bad attitudes, talking of corners to be cut, improvements to be made, all the time interacting. But this is not training. Rather, it's just a manifestation of a human instinct to look, speak and learn. Side-by-side training takes that instinct, and uses and develops it, as you'll see.

Creating an Environment for Side-by-side Training

Side-by-side training, by its nature, is more intimate than most. By the same token, some might say 'more intimidating'. Given the implications of side-by-side training, what should be the prevailing management, staff and organizational attitudes to make side-by-side training work?

Here are our thoughts.

Management Attitudes

By definition, side-by-side training takes place at work, and usually in the line. That means that there's a possibility that side-by-side training will disrupt and slow down productive work.

That makes it crucial for managers to regard the provision of training and support **as part of their jobs**. Moving managers away from the idea that 'The training department does training' and gaining their commitment to the more enlightened, participative view isn't easy, but it's worth the effort. We'll suggest some ways of doing it later in this section.

Staff Attitudes

The side-by-side trainer is often a more experienced or senior colleague. So staff as well as managers need to see training as a line responsibility. But you really need more than that. Ideally, your coaches should take pride in their ability to develop more junior staff and actually enjoy it.

Organizational Attitudes

The organization as a whole also needs to be committed to training in the line. But at an organizational level this commitment needs to go further. Increasingly, successful organizations are seeing training and development as a career-long process for their staff. Organizations with that kind of philosophy will expect a high standard of side-by-side training, will develop people to provide it and make available the necessary resources for it to happen.

So, what can we do to encourage these attitudes and create this environment? We need to start by finding out what things are like now. For instance, if managers, staff and the organization see training as the responsibility of the the training department, we need to find out why. Often it's because the trainers have been scared to let anyone else involve themselves in the training in case it did them out of a job. In that case, the first attitude to change is that of the trainers. After that, there are two actions needed, the one related to **philosophy** and the other to **practice**.

We shall start with the **philosophical**. Seek to achieve a policy statement with a first line which reads:

> *'Managers are responsible for the training and development of their staff.'*

Once this is in place, you should set about a process of internal marketing. If you can get the senior members of your organization to make the point in staff newspapers, the annual report, on notice boards and anywhere else you can think of, the message will start to spread. If the bosses are saying it, people will take notice when you repeat it. But they must start the ball rolling.

The second action is extremely **practical**. It involves a subtle mix of publicity and training:

- You need to introduce workshops for every manager, supervisor and potential coach who may be affected by this new emphasis on side-by-side training.
  The training is there to make sure everyone feels confident and capable of making it work.
- The publicity is to do with telling people **why** this is happening: what will the benefits be?

Then, having won the internal marketing war, you can turn to detailed implementation.

Choosing and Developing Coaches

Given the nature of coaching — what kind of people would you seek to take over the role? Write your answers here.

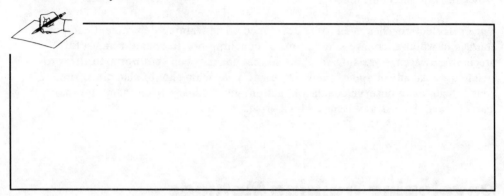

In our experience, the most skilled people at a task are often not the best people to teach it. That's because they've been doing it for so long, instinctively, that they don't know how they do it any more and just can't understand how anybody could find difficulty with any part of it.

So, for us, the best coaches:

- do the job following a conscious and logical routine
- are able to analyse the job into manageable chunks
- can still remember the time when they found it difficult
- enjoy explaining their skill
- get a kick out of helping others to learn.

Coaches who meet these standards will need searching for, but you may be pleasantly surprised at what you find when you go out to look.

The important thing to recognize is that the coach is above all a **facilitator** — making it easy for other people to learn. So the key part of the coach's job is to get the learner going — and so learning by doing — as soon as possible.

That means that good coaches are prepared to keep quiet even when learners are struggling. It's about encouraging and reassuring learners; providing practical reinforcement. It's about recognizing that side-by-side training means giving people an opportunity to learn for themselves, not filling them up with what the coaches know. Above all, perhaps, it's about being able to withdraw gently as the learner grows in skill and confidence.

Once selected, coaches need to be developed. The training department can put on courses in which there are simulations of coaching practice, and, as a useful precursor, awareness-raising sessions so that coaches can spot **opportunities** to coach and take advantage of them. You and your team should also allow time in your schedules to observe coaches in action, get feedback from them **and** their learners, and discuss any issues which arise.

Developing Training Methods

The coaching skills we have talked about so far are more to do with managing people than managing training. We do not see coaches as skilled instructional designers — that's not their job. So effective coaching in part depends on your ability to provide easy-to-use source material, which we think should come from the centre. The sort of things we have in mind are:

- trainer notes which give clear instructions to the coach on how to run the session
- clear indication of timing (if appropriate)
- details of how to obtain necessary resources
- basic indicators to evaluate the success of the coaching.

This kind of material can be used in several different ways:

- training department issues a training calendar and the training support material goes out in advance of each designated session

- training department issues a catalogue of training support materials and specifies which should be used when

- training department issues a catalogue of training support materials and leaves line managers to decide what is relevant when.

You will recall what we said earlier about getting the line to accept responsibility for training. The closer you can come to the situation where line management tells **you** what materials it needs and the objectives they are to meet, the healthier side-by-side training will be in your organization.

Assessment and Monitoring

We must start by recognizing that there is a major difference between side-by-side training and most other forms of training. The difference is that the quality of other forms of training — course, open learning, CBT — is largely under the control of the training department. While the training department can provide materials for side-by-side training and train coaches, it has no control over what happens in the coaching sessions. The result is a need for information about three things:

- how good and relevant the training support material itself is

- how well it is being delivered

- what the result of the coaching has been.

Good, relevant material should have been designed for delivery by trained coaches, to achieve specific performance objectives. So a key aspect of your assessment process will involve objective and subjective feedback from the coaches about both the training itself and the performance of their learners. Equally valid would be feedback from learners about both the materials and the coaching process.

The question, of course, is how, practically, do you get this information. This will depend on the structure, geographical dispersion, culture and reporting systems of your organization. But whatever the case, one or more of the following methods will be appropriate:

- written questionnaires
- discussion groups
- individual interviews
- practical tests
- written tests
- checklists covering the main descriptors and key indicators of objectives.

The more objective indicators — like checklists — would provide a profile of achievement across the organization, and help you identify areas of higher or lower achievement. The same information would tell you the content of the coaching in different areas of the organization. You would also know who has been coached, and by whom. Increasing levels of achievement against personal or team objectives would testify to the skills which have been effectively acquired.

This is the kind of information you need in order to maintain and renew your training strategy. In the end, the means by which you gain this information is a matter for you and the organization in which you operate.

Summary

Reading through Chapter 2, you started with a brief analysis of what is involved in side-by-side training. Far from being something which happens spontaneously and which you can ignore, effective side-by-side training needs your closest attention. You have to take advantage of the natural human inclination to look, speak and learn. This means, in practice:

- creating an environment where side-by-side training can flourish
- choosing and developing coaches
- developing training methods
- assessing and monitoring progress.

The environment in which side-by-side training flourishes is one where attitudes in your organization are basically sound: managers, staff and the organization itself need to be properly in tune with the spirit of effective side-by-side training. Ensuring this is so will involve you in some internal marketing of the idea that training is part of every manager's job and a key responsibility.

On the theme of assessment and monitoring, you need to know:

* how good and relevant the training support material which you've developed is
* how well it has been delivered
* how successful the coaching has been.

You looked at a number of ways of obtaining this information.

Choosing and developing coaches is a skilled task. The best coaches work to a logical routine, can analyse their job into manageable chunks and enjoy explaining it. Basically, they're sympathetic people rather than people with large amounts of technical expertise. They will none the less need your support as they coach — you should plan time to observe them and discuss their techniques.

Then it comes to materials, you saw that this is very much a task for you and your team to undertake, but in close collaboration with line managers.

Assignment:

Use the headings and sub-headings you've seen in this chapter to make a checklist. Pick one area of side-by-side training which is current or planned in your organization and write down against each item on the checklist:

- *what you do at the various stages of planning, implementing and monitoring the training.*

Leave some space against each item so that you can write down during and after the training:

- *how that particular aspect of your input into the side-by-side training went*
- *what (if anything) you would do differently next time.*

You will notice that this assignment eventually builds into an action plan for you to follow throughout your preparation for all future side-by-side training.

Text-based Open Learning

There is such a thing as 'direct learning', also called 'learning through experience', or 'learning through pain': it teaches you, very graphically, that fire is hot, ice is slippery and so on. There is a time and a place for such learning, but the difficulty, almost impossibility, of controlling it effectively rules it out of the trainer's repertoire. So there always needs to be some kind of medium for training, which can select, refine and present training in an appropriate way. As we have already seen with group-based training and side-by-side training, that medium can be a person — a teacher or a trainer. But there are other effective media for the presentation of training, too. We shall look at text first.

By the time you have completed this chapter, you will be able to:

- define open learning, and describe its advantages and drawbacks
- describe how best to source your open learning
- state how best to update your materials
- identify the most appropriate support for learners
- state the details which should be monitored and recorded.

Why Text-based Open Learning?

Well researched and written open learning text is a proven, highly effective medium for teaching new skills and effecting their transfer to practice in the workplace. Although the cost of developing text can be relatively high, it does not approach the giddy heights of the more sophisticated of cutting edge technology. The classic situation in which text-based learning scores highly is where there is a large learning population, which of course, brings unit costs tumbling. Geographic dispersal of that population also presents no problems to text-based learning. Text is easily updatable to keep all the information current but, perhaps most important, it puts responsibility for learning into the hands of each individual learner. The choice of how, when and where to work is particularly apposite in an organization which is serious about individual responsibilities and accountabilities.

How to Choose Suitable Materials

If you are choosing open learning text 'off-the-shelf', there are some very important judgements you must make about the material before you commit people and money to it.

Is the Material Relevant to Your Needs?

There are two broad approaches to choosing off-the-shelf text. One goes: 'We could do with some more communication in our place, so I'll give them a text about it'. This could be called a hit-and-miss approach — though the likelihood is, it will be more miss than hit.

Or, you could have carried out your training needs analysis and identified the learning objectives appropriate for the target audience. You can then match your objectives with those set out in the open learning text. The closer the match, the more likely you are to have found what you need.

Check, too, that the text provides:

- regular activities for learning reinforcement
- regular assessment, so learners and trainers can evaluate the training
- regular summaries of key points
- constant reference to day-to-day practice in the workplace

- clear layout and unambiguous language to smooth the learning process
- lots of support for learners, particularly in responses to activities.

So, having matched your objectives with those of the text, you might feel you are home and dry. Or are you?

What else do you think you should consider before putting your training budget into text-based open learning? Write your answer here.

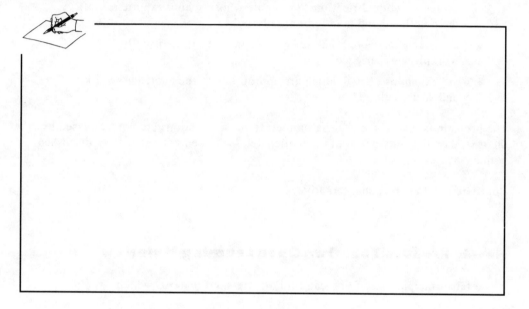

We believe that you should always take your people's perspective into account in training matters — and open learning is no exception. The main factor to consider is whether the material is appropriate to your people.

Is the Material Appropriate to Your People?

Even material which **you** judge matches your organization's needs can fail — if it does not engage with its audience. So first of all, **you** need to know that audience pretty well. Ask some questions about the general characteristics of the workforce:

- what style, reading level and vocabulary will be right for them?
- to what level or depth is the subject treated?
- are they likely to be seasoned learners, with a degree or professional qualifications, or people whose school experience left them deflated and glad to be rid of books?
- are examples quoted that make sense in terms of their daily workplace experience?
- are examples quoted which are appropriate to the audience's work and social culture?

The problem is that, if the criteria implicit in those questions are not addressed by the text, then the audience could feel alienated — 'talked at', rather than 'discussed with'.

But there is, of course, an alternative.

How to Produce Your Own Open Learning Materials

It is a fair principle that, if you can find off-the-shelf material which:

- meets your organization's needs
- meets trainee's learning needs
- is within your budget . . .

. . . you should buy it.

Sometimes these 'generic' texts will meet **some** of the needs of **some** of your people, leaving you to top-up as appropriate.

There are three ways to put in place the open learning text you need.

Write Study Guides

Imagine a circumstance in which you have all the required **learning content** in your resource centre. There are bits in, say, reference works, workbooks, videos, workplace legislation — but nothing packaged and prepared for learning.

The effective study guide will:

- identify material which meets your learning objectives
- reference and introduce that material
- guide the learner to the material
- relate the materials to the reality of workplace activity
- set appropriate activities
- provide regular summaries
- keep the learner aware of their achievement.

A word of warning — if you regard producing study guides as a soft option, you will get it wrong. Well-produced study guides will organize and enhance your existing training resources. Badly produced ones will compromise them — possibly terminally.

Write Open Learning Text

You might decide that the size of your audience and the uniqueness of its needs leads you to set up your own open learning section. This requires full-time writers and appropriate reprographic support. It is important to understand that not everybody can be a writer. In many ways, the worst person to write open learning text is the subject expert. They are too close to what they know and can do, and tend to make assumptions on other people's behalf. Make sure that all your writers are trained in open learning techniques.

The advantages of having your own open learning section are considerable, though. You can ensure that the workbooks are absolutely right for the organization's and individual's needs. They can also act as a vehicle for company culture — and market the training department in all parts of the organization.

Use an External Consultant

Consider an external consultant if you're convinced you want to use open learning, but do not want to commit to establishing a permanent, in-house unit.

The right consultant will bring plenty of expertise to the job, and undertake to produce what you need within a limited number of drafts.

The consultant will want to work **with** you, finding out about the organization, its needs, your aims and objectives, and the target audience, and will seek to test the materials before final publication.

But do remember, it is your responsibility to give the consultant a briefing which is complete, accurate and unambiguous. That is the only way to get what you need out of the process.

Updating Open Learning Materials

There are some themes and subjects which are unlikely to need updating. Basic material about communication or motivation theory will not change significantly, but in-house procedures, documentation or legislation can change with irritating frequency. You will need a method for updating your open learning text. So . . .

- classify your texts, so you can find them easily
- mark each update, so you know which is the latest version
- have a system to let people know that updates have happened
- package your learning to make updating easy:
  — use loose-leaf folders, so updated pages can be slotted in
  — issue amendment stickers
  — as texts become redundant, throw them away.

Supporting Learners

Research shows that high quality open learning can fail if it is not properly supported, whereas even mediocre material can succeed to a certain degree if it is well supported.

The kind of support required can broadly be classified as **technical** and **emotional** support.

Give three or four examples of each type of support. Put your answers in the box.

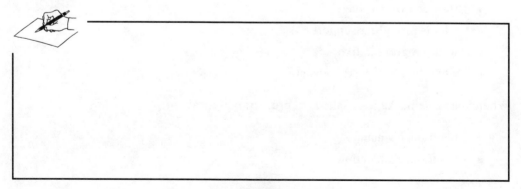

Technical support revolves around the material itself or its content, so technical support would involve:

- letting people know where learning material is
- letting people know how to use the material
- providing human support (line manager, mentors, etc.)
- providing a telephone helpline
- ensuring regular feedback.

Emotional support is just as necessary as technical support. People need to know what they are doing wrong — or even more importantly, what they are doing right. They need to learn in a blame-free culture, and be listened to when things go wrong at home and interrupt their learning. Face-to-face contact with an understanding mentor will provide this support. The mentor could be a trainer, colleague, supervisor or manager. The rank doesn't matter. The character and style do.

Monitoring Open Learning

Precisely because open learning is so good with large populations of learners, it is easy to lose touch with what is happening. Information should be kept on:

- **who** is undertaking **what** package
- start and finish times
- who is providing support
- what progress is like
- what the likely next steps are.

When you issue packages, make a record, straight away, of:

- the trainee's name
- the trainee's location

- the trainee's manager
- package details.

Then you can keep in touch with that manager on the trainee's progress. You could develop a paper-based system recording all relevant details on a regular basis, to be administered by the appropriate manager, supervisor or mentor.

All this information should provide hard data, such as:

- which learners are excelling in their scheme of study
- which learners are having difficulties
- which packages are particularly successful
- which packages have elements which need to be improved
- how long packages are taking to work through
- how effective the support systems are being.

Summary

In Chapter 3, you saw the key points relating to how you implement text-based open learning, namely:

- the features which make open learning suitable for use in your organization and how best to provide the appropriate open learning
- ways and means of creating your own open learning resource bank
- the difficulties associated with updating open learning texts and how to combat them
- the nature of the support you should provide
- the records you should keep.

Assignment:

Use the headings and sub-headings you've seen in this chapter to make a checklist. Pick one area of training through open learning which is planned in your organization and write down against each item on the checklist:

- *what you do at the various stages of planning, implementing and monitoring the training.*

Leave some space after each item so that you can write down during and after the training:

- *how that particular aspect of your input into the open learning went*
- *what (if anything) you would do differently next time.*

You will notice that this assignment eventually builds into an action plan for you to follow throughout your preparation for all future open learning in your organization.

Computer-based Training and Interactive Video

Do not let go of what you have just read about text-based open learning, because both computer-based training (CBT) and interactive video (IV) are only **technological ways of delivering open learning**. This chapter will deal with questions peculiar to these high tech media, or which take on an extra dimension because of them.

By the time you have completed this chapter, you will be able to:

- list factors to consider about delivery systems
- describe the situations in which CBT and IV will work best
- show how to select and develop programmes
- identify the specific kind of support CBT and IV require.

Before we move on, though, a word about cost.

Cost

CBT and IV will be costly because:

- commercial programmes are expensive
- in-house programmes take a long time to develop
- authoring and delivery system will inevitably be sophisticated.

Also bear in mind that this high cost means you must have a coherent strategy involving both the training department and its customers from the line. The reason is that the costs for high tech training are both high and visible. Generally, training costs will come out of the training department's budget. But with high tech training it is more likely that costs will be shared, say between the training department and the line — and that will need approval at a strategic level.

Delivery Systems

We reckon there are two main questions to address about delivery systems:

- What sort?
- Where?

What Sort of Delivery System?

To answer this question, you need answers to a few other questions first. For instance:

- What is your organization's preferred computer platform: PC compatible, Apple, or UNIX?

It is important to produce training programmes which are compatible with the hardware your organization already uses. You may still incur hardware costs, but this way you'll keep them to a minimum.

- How does your organization currently provide computer services?

The answer to this question will fall somewhere on a spectrum which has 'central mainframe' at one end to 'desk-top computers' at the other. Go and talk to your computer specialists about ways of piggy-backing CBT, IV, or both on to your organization's existing communications technology. If there's already been a significant investment in this technology, it's only sensible to make use of it.

- Do you have a network?

A communications network will allow you to store CBT programmes in a central computer and transmit them to terminals elsewhere when required. This offers clear advantages in storage capacity, an updating facility and ease of access to learner records and performance. If there's no network, you can still deliver CBT — it's more expensive and inconvenient, that's all.

Armed with answers to these questions, you can now start to design your delivery system. Do remember the cost implications of what you're doing, though. We know of one major organization which installed a very sophisticated delivery system for CBT only to find 18 months later that it was too limited in capacity. They chose to rip it all out and start again, but it cost them several millions. The decisions you make now will affect what you can do over the next few years — so make them wisely.

Where Will the Hardware be Located?

As we've said, CBT and IV are no more than open learning with knobs on. So we need to remember the benefits of open learning in terms of ease of use and ready availability. But when we think about where to put the hardware, we need to keep this consideration of convenience on one side of the balance and cost on the other. In our experience, access to CBT and IV should be quick and easy. The choice you make depends, of course, on the nature of your organization and the budget available. But, wherever possible, we'd like to see the hardware going out to the learners, not the learner coming in to the hardware. This means that keeping CBT and IV in the centre can be the least effective answer. Local access centres are better and CBT on everyone's desk is better still.

Suitable Subjects

The big advantage that CBT and IV have over text-based open learning is that they are genuinely interactive. When we asked you to think about issues in this book, we had to guess your answers and respond according to our guesses. But with CBT and IV, particularly of the more sophisticated, branching variety, the learner gets a response which will differ according to their answers.

A further advantage is that you can make images on the screen — computer graphics with CBT, high-quality video with IV.

The worst thing that can be done with CBT and IV is to ignore the technological advantages they have over other media. Too often we have seen CBT in particular do no more than electronically turn pages. Screen after screen of text, with an activity every now and then, does not justify the rejection of text for technology! If you are going to opt for CBT or IV, be sure you know why you are doing it.

Given these unique features of CBT and IV, what subjects do you think lend themselves to high tech treatment? Answers in the box, please.

The obvious answer is anything that will fully exploit CBT's and IV's unique capabilities — and equally, to reject for CBT and IV anything that text could handle equally as well.

For instance, high tech training really scores where you ask the trainee about an advisable course of action, and the programme can show the consequences. CBT and IV can cope with multiple answers to questions, and so are excellent for getting over the idea of responsibility for events, and accountability. In brief, they can show how actions A, B or C could have consequences X, Y or Z.

These two high tech media are also very helpful when the learner is to be involved in a practical skill. With a computer display, the learner can fill in forms, add-up numbers, write memos for the programme to comment on, etc. With a video sequence, he or she can watch a technical operation or a role-play and dictate what happens next by answering questions or choosing alternatives.

Selecting and Developing Programmes

The principles of CBT and IV are now well developed, and you can find some pretty spectacular programmes. But what are to be your criteria for buying into high tech training?

If you decide to go down the track of buying commercial CBT or IV programmes, our advice would be the same as for open learning texts:

- set clear learning objectives — so you know what you want the programme to do

- look for a good match with the style and level of your target group

- check the instructional design — that it will lead to learning and, consequently, performance gains

- be sure that the programmes do more than text can do — otherwise stick with text.

In addition, do make sure the written instructions are comprehensible! Most CBT and IV programmes are written by computer specialists who may overlook the fact that some of us have trouble with light switches, let alone disc drives.

Check, too, that any accompanying support material (often text-based) meets your quality and other criteria.

People

For efficient CBT development, you'll need a minimum of two people: a designer and a programmer. For IV, you'll need to add a director and an editor. That assumes your CBT designer can also write film scripts.

Most importantly, remember that high quality pictures and slick direction will **not** cover up weak ideas — in fact, they will probably throw them into sharp relief. The principle of rubbish in, rubbish out holds good. Programmers and writers must be aware of the capacity of these training media, and exploit that capacity to the full. There is no excuse for programmes that are static and dull.

Technical Support

Everything we said about text-based open learning and the need for technical support applies equally to CBT and IV. But CBT and IV need something additional by way of technical support.

Identify some details of the technical support CBT and IV will need.

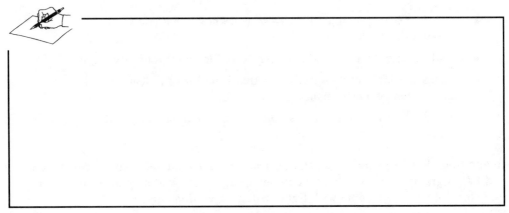

The straightforward answer to this one is what we might more accurately call 'technological support'. In some cases, learners using CBT and IV may not normally be involved with computers, monitors, floppy discs, video disc players or the yards of cable that tie the whole lot together. That makes it important to ensure that the technology doesn't get in the way of the learning. So, for CBT and IV, technical support needs to include someone close at hand who can, if need be, explain where the on-off switch is, how to load the programme, what to do if the screen won't light up and provide solutions to the million and one problems which afflict the technologically naive.

This support may come in the form of a telephone hotline or a personal service, but it must be there. You can be pretty sure that any attempt to introduce CBT or IV without it will initially draw a hostile response, and ultimately fail.

Postscript — Compact Disc Interactive

CD-i is increasingly becoming a significant player in the world of high tech training.

CD-i contains all the values of CBT and Interactive Video. You can save film, cartoon, stills, sound and text on the disc, and use all these to present realistic scenarios for the trainee to react to. The delivery systems are portable and affordable. The flexibility is almost infinite, and the ability to create on disc real work conditions is impressive.

Apply the same criteria to selecting CD-i as you would to any other form of high tech training — though a word of warning. CD-i is still very expensive indeed to develop — but it might be the medium to meet your needs.

Summary

Chapter 4 showed you the central issues relating to your use of CBT or IV, and other technologically sophisticated training media.

First there was an explanation of what can make the costs of high tech training prohibitive in certain circumstances.

We then moved on to explain the different ways in which the training can be 'delivered' to the trainee.

The next point in the chapter was the different ways in which CBT and allied training media need support from people with specific skills in the organization, both in producing the training materials and ensuring that they are used appropriately and effectively.

Assignment:

Use the headings and sub-headings you've seen in this chapter to make a checklist. Pick one area of training through CBT or IV which is planned in your organization and write down against each item on the checklist:

- *what you do at the various stages of planning, implementing and monitoring the training.*

Leave some space after each item so that you can write down during and after the training:

- *how that particular aspect of your input into the CBT/IV went*
- *what (if anything) you would do differently next time.*

You will notice that this assignment eventually builds into an action plan for you to follow throughout your preparation for all future high-technology training in your organization.

Discovery Learning

Discovery learning is one of the most natural forms of learning there is. It taps into a person's instincts to acquire knowledge and skills and, if you implement it correctly, you will be able to foster in the learner appropriate attitudes to work as well.

By the time you've completed this chapter, you'll be able to:

- define a suitable task, project or problem for learners to tackle
- take learners out of their normal work environment to confront the training task
- give learners access to sources of knowledge or skill to apply to the project
- build-in regular tutorial reviews and support
- enable learners to benefit from their learning on return to their normal jobs.

You're now going to consider the practical actions needed to achieve these objectives. The theory of discovery learning is fairly straightforward, so we don't intend to add much here to what we said about it in *Selecting Training Methods*. Basically it is about presenting individuals or small groups of learners with tasks or projects taken from real life and running in real time, and supporting them as they learn by 'discovery' what the correct approach is. In our view, though, the challenge is to set up discovery learning so that the learner sees it as:

- real
- relevant
- stimulating
  and
- of long-term benefit.

So, as we work through the five stages listed, we'll be asking you to consider them from our favourite standpoint, that of the **customer**.

Defining Tasks and Projects

From the learner's standpoint, what would constitute a meaningful discovery learning project? Write your answer here.

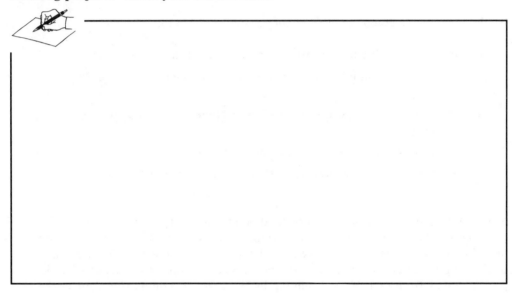

In our experience, discovery learners have derived most 'meaning' from their experience where:

- the task was real
- the solutions were real and practicable
- the learners were able to justify their solutions in front of people who really know what the solution should be.

So we reckon that the best kind of discovery learning project is the **real problem** that's been left lying around because there was no one to tackle it. We live in an imperfect world, so we'd be surprised if your organization didn't have at least a few problems needing solutions.

After that, it's a question of matching the **scale of the problem** with the seniority of the people, the numbers of people involved and the time-scale of the project. Too small a problem will lead to learners learning nothing of significance. Too big a problem will result in them giving up. A mistake in either direction will mean the project doesn't meet the all-important criteria of relevance, stimulation and long-term benefit.

Case Study

Ben Jolliffe Associates took on a new open learning writer to meet increased demand for their materials. The newcomer — Ivan Scrafton — had a background in education and publishing and knew a fair bit about instructional design, but the rigours of working on a project were uncharted territory for him, so discovery learning was deemed to be the way forward. There was on the books a real 'old chestnut' of a project which had for several reasons never actually been developed, but neither had it been abandoned. The client was keen to progress the matter, Ben Jolliffe himself wanted his shelves cleared of all loose ends — of which this was the most obvious — so the solution was to give the project to the new starter as discovery learning.

Ivan finished the project in two weeks to the complete satisfaction of all concerned. Most importantly, his own levels of self-confidence in his abilities to run a project and deal with clients were sky-high, and he went on to become a respected member of the team.

Freeing Learners to Learn

From the learner's standpoint, what actions are needed to give freedom to undertake the project? Write them, in sequence where appropriate, in this box.

Our answer to this is a bit back-to-front, because we've been thinking about all the things which can — and do — intervene to stop people learning. Things like:

- urgent requests to ring the office
- forwarding post for attention
- visits from line managers
- out-of-hours meetings.

These and similar events are all ways of saying, 'The discovery learning project can take a back seat; your learning isn't really important'. If that's the way discovery learning projects are viewed in your organization, you'd best give them up altogether, or prepare yourself for some hard work to change people's perceptions. Here are some things you might do to ensure that these distractions do not occur, and so the learners are free to learn during the course of the task or project:

- set up briefings so that everyone knows how discovery learning is supposed to operate
- carry out individual briefings for the reporting managers and the learners on a specific project
- arrange proper cover for the learner's job during the project
- involve managers in project reviews so that they develop a sense of ownership — they'll be less likely to interrupt projects they've agreed to support
- sell the learning benefits so that managers are committed to a project's success.

Providing Resources

Discovery learners need human and paper resources — sometimes in copious quantities, so it's as well to anticipate this need: look at our four headings, and you'll get an idea of the sort of thing to expect.

We saw possible resources being people or paper, internal or external.

- **Internal people** would come from any level or any function that's relevant to the project

- **External people** could be suppliers, customers, analysts, researchers, academics, bankers or any other kind of relevant expert

- **Internal paper** could be an archive, a database, accounts, customer records, manuals or procedures

- **External paper** could be a general library, a specialist library, government records, other official data, industrial statistics or a whole range of other possibilities.

The trainer's involvement with all or any of these is to:

- decide which resources are relevant and potentially useful

- advise learners of the possibilities

- obtain access which may mean anything from arranging library tickets to booking appointments

- act as fixer of appointments or a facilitator. This means responding to learner requests for resources. The learners need to feel that the project is theirs, to take in any direction they choose. They shouldn't feel manipulated by the trainer, which is what will happen if all the appointments are pre-booked and the trainer insists on them being kept. The most helpful thing the trainer can do is to act as secretary to the individual or group so that they can concentrate on their learning.

Reviewing Progress

What progress would you want to review as a learner? And what progress
would you want to review as a trainer? Write your answers in here.

There's a potential for conflict between what learners and trainees want to get out of the review process. Typically, if the project is well designed and resourced, learners will be hooked on achieving their objective. So the progress they want to review will be **progress towards that objective.**

For trainers, on the other hand, the project itself should be secondary. Of course, it's important for the group and the organization that a solution should be found to the problem. But the trainers' priority ought to be **the learning process**. The learners won't be tackling the same project again. That makes the project a convenient vehicle for learning other skills, not an end in itself.

And, of course, there's a third party interested in the project — the problem-owner. His or her perspective is also slightly different. While the learners will want a solution as near to perfect as possible and the trainers will want an effective learning vehicle, the problem-owner will want a quick, cheap and easy solution. That, after all, is the way things are.

So the trainer needs to reconcile and satisfy all of these conflicting demands on the review process. A good place to start is with the recognition that you'll need to make an effort to get any reviews happening at all. They won't take place naturally. That in turn is part of a wider process which encourages learners to spend a lot of time at the **start** of a project considering:

- objectives
- standards of performance
- activities
- time-scales
- resource requirements
- progress checking.

At the start of a project, learners will welcome all the guidance they can get. If you arrange times and dates for reviews at this stage, they will become an accepted part of the process. As the project gathers momentum, it will become increasingly difficult to add another item to the timetable which the learners will see filling up at an alarming rate.

It's also important to differentiate at the planning stage between reviews of the **project** (progress towards objectives) and of the **process** (what people are learning). As the project rolls on learners will argue that they don't have time to review the process. If you attempt to review progress and process together, the former will squeeze out the latter. If follows that progress and process reviews must be timetabled **separately** from the outset.

You may have gathered from what we've said so far that process reviews aren't the easiest thing in the world to sell to your learner. Whether you succeed in selling them will depend very much on how the learners perceive you. We said earlier that the trainer should act as a fixer/facilitator — if you've succeeded in that role, learners will be prepared to trust and take notice of you. Relevant support and guidance in other aspects of the project will make you credible when it comes to suggesting process reviews.

And, finally, how to involve the problem-owner. That starts with the brief you give your learners. It needs to be agreed with the problem-owner and to state, very clearly, not only the problem to be solved but also the constraints within which the solution must fall:

- cost
- equipment
- people
- time
- disruptions, and so on.

Set out like this, the brief will make it valuable to both the problem-owner and the learners if they review progress together. Of course the problem-owner shouldn't be included in every review, but regular involvement will benefit both parties.

The Re-entry Problem

What support would you need as a learner to enable you to apply what you've learnt from a project to your own job? Write your answer here.

We've already answered this question in a slightly haphazard fashion in other parts of this book. The support we think a learner would need includes:

- a sympathetic and comprehensive briefing from a manager who understands the project
- detailed action plans
- regular reviews against plan deadlines
- job-related activities which make specific use of the project learning
- at worst, possible transfer to a job where the learner can apply more of the skills he or she has learnt.

We'd like to round off this section on discovery learning by developing that last point a bit further. An effective project will give learners a very different outlook on their jobs, their future career, the organization and the nature of management. You shouldn't then be surprised if some of those who have been through the process find it difficult to settle back into their old routines. Discovery learning is a powerful experience. Organizations need to be flexible to cope with its results.

Summary

In the course of this chapter you have seen the major points relating to the implementation of discovery learning.

First, you saw the challenges involved in finding the right task or project to be the subject of the training.

After that, you saw the need to free the learner to learn — which means identifying and then neutralizing all possible distractions.

The next stage was to provide the necessary resources — and we divided resources up into external and internal, people and paper.

Moving on, the next challenge to meet was the need to review progress — and you saw just what the review is supposed to achieve, and methods of enabling it to do so.

The last, but very important point was the challenge of closely tying in what's been learned with the real world of work. We called this re-entry — a phrase deliberately chosen to highlight the possible gap between the training and what may be a more mundane working reality.

Assignment:

Use the headings and sub-headings you've seen in this chapter to make a checklist. Pick one area of discovery learning which is planned in your organization and write down against each item on the checklist:

- *what you do at the various stages of planning, implementing and monitoring the training — including especially what you do to tie the training into reality.*

Leave some space after each item so that you can write down during and after the training:

- *how that particular aspect of your input into the discovery learning went*
- *what (if anything) you would do differently next time.*

You will notice that this assignment eventually builds into an action plan for you to follow throughout your preparation for all future discovery learning in your organization.

Further Reading

A Practical Approach to Group Training
D Leigh Kogan Page 1991

One-to-One Training and Coaching Skills
Buckley and Caple Kogan Page 1991

Effective Use of Role-Play
Morry van Ments Kogan Page 1989

Mutimedia Computer Assisted Learning
Philip Barker Kogan Page 1989

Learning in Groups
David Jaques Kogan Page 1991